THE GIFTS OF LOVE

Trusting, caring, sharing—these are the gifts of love and friendship that we all seek and yet shy away from in today's world.

In this book, *When Lovers Are Friends*, Merle Shain offers wise and warm words for the greatest emotional dilemma of our times: fear of intimacy and commitment, and our seemingly contradictory fear of loneliness.

Filled with reassuring insights, *When Lovers Are Friends* is like a letter from a close and compassionate friend.

- How can we find love—
the right kind of love for us—
and keep it flourishing?

- How can we achieve greater
self-acceptance and find ways to
produce love so that it grows
from us instead of being consumed?

MERLE SHAIN
WHEN LOVERS ARE FRIENDS

"Lovers really can be friends, and Merle Shain tells us all about it in this unusually charming and insightful book."—Theodore I. Rubin, M.D.

Bantam Books by Merle Shain

SOME MEN ARE MORE PERFECT THAN OTHERS
WHEN LOVERS ARE FRIENDS

WHEN LOVERS ARE FRIENDS

MERLE SHAIN

BANTAM BOOKS · TORONTO · NEW YORK · LONDON

WHEN LOVERS ARE FRIENDS

*A Bantam Book / published by arrangement with
J. B. Lippincott Company*

PRINTING HISTORY

*J. B. Lippincott edition published September 1978
Book-Of-The-Month Club edition published November 1978
Macmillan Book Club edition published March 1979
Serialized in Working Woman Magazine, June 1979 issue
Bantam edition / September 1979*

Photograph of Merle Shain by Garry Gross.

ISBN 0-553-01203-7

PRINTED IN THE UNITED STATES OF AMERICA

0 9 8 7 6 5 4 3 2 1

For my friends
whom I need not name
as they know who they are and
what they mean to me

Contents

Part One

TRUSTING

*It is a long time
since I have asked heaven for anything,
but still my arms will not come down.*
ANTONIO PORCHIA

1

Caring can cost a lot, but not caring always costs more

I had a confidant once, a friend who was older and wiser and knew much more about life, and through a long and awful year I poured my heart out to her and she gave me her advice. I told her of the man I loved, and of how he was deceiving me, and she listened to my stories and told me what to do. And after I had lost him, and after she had been divorced, I came to learn the man who'd been my love had been her lover too, and when I turned on her with shock, she told me that I'd seduced her with my tales of love, and that it was because of me she'd left her marriage bed.

It's been many years since this happened, and years since either of us had any hope of being loved by him, but I still hear her words and ask myself if she was right. And while I know most would say she stole my man from me and took advantage of my trust, and that the sin was hers, not mine, still part of me knows you can be guilty even while you're innocent, and that I am as much to blame.

I don't know what prompted me to tell this story now after so many years have passed, but I suspect it is because it seems to say, better than any other way I know, that lives that touch, touch many ways, and relationships are very complex things with many currents in the tide. And though I know one never means to hurt, I know as well that all those who love both laugh and weep.

There has been a lot of talk about independence lately, about the cost of sharing your life, and many people feel that caring costs too much. We are all afraid of being swallowed up by love, of ceasing to exist except through someone else, so we rush toward love with open arms and hide from it when it comes to us. And we ask ourselves a hundred times if the cost of love is not too high, while we juggle our needs for self and love like two hot balls. We can't hold long to either one.

There can be a lot of hurt in love, and there is always risk, and one can't help wondering sometimes if there couldn't be a better way to live. Most of us have asked ourselves that question more than once. The trouble is that the pain in love is mixed with the joy and good, and there is no way to separate them out. You take them both or you get nothing at all. And one never really knows when you start up with someone whether you should open your arms to them or shut them firmly out.

Once they have been hurt by love, many people never trust again, never venture fully out in life with an open heart. And many of them hedge their bets ever after and feel that life's a cheat and trap, until what they fear most in time comes to pass.

Love is short, forgetting's long, and understanding takes longer still. And sometimes it is hard to know what someone has given us, or even what we have given them, until a long time after the event. But if I'm to tell you everything there is to tell, I have to tell you this—the friend who shared that man with me taught me about myself, and I have that today while neither of us has him. So who is there to say she was not my friend or that all friends must be safe? Maybe it's only important that we love and learn.

There have been a lot of books about self-love lately, about doing your own thing and being yourself, and those who talk of understanding, of intimacy, or love, talk largely to themselves. It is easy when you've been hurt by love to give it up as a bad job and make independence your new god, taking the love you had to give and turning it in upon yourself. And most of us have had to protect ourselves so much at times that we've given up the high road and taken the low. But independence carried to the furthest extreme is just loneliness and death, nothing more than another defense, and there is no growth in it, only a safe harbor for a while. The answer doesn't lie in learning how to protect ourselves from life—it lies in learning how to become strong enough to let a bit more of it in. And that is the direction in which I am myself trying to head.

I know that many people feel they have to draw away, and others so damaged from the wars can never fight again. I know the joys of owning yourself. I have sung that song myself. But dimly and from a hidden place, I hear a most insistent voice saying to anyone who wants to hear, "There is no growth without love."

There is a difference between an independence which comes from strength and one which is a retreat from life, the retrenchment of a spirit not trusting in itself. And while I know we are all afraid of being hurt and take two steps back for every forward one we take, the truth is the moment when we are most ourselves is when we reach out and answer the call from someone else.

It is very difficult to accept the fact that there are no guarantees in life, no guarantees that life will progress as it should or that the people you care about will love you back, or even that they will treat you right. But trust in life does not mean trusting that life will always be good or that it will be free of grief and pain. It means trusting that somewhere inside yourself you can find the strength to go forth and meet what comes and, even if you meet betrayal and disappointment along the way, go forth again the very next day.

The Eskimos have a legend about the caribou and the wolf. The caribou and the wolf are one, they say. The caribou feeds the wolf but the wolf keeps the caribou strong. And so it is with people, too. There are people to be soft with and people who make you strong. There are those who protect you and those who teach you to protect yourself. There are people whom you trusted and, when you couldn't, found how to trust yourself. And if you are lucky there is something to be gained from each.

"Man is born broken," Eugene O'Neill wrote in *The Great God Brown*. "He lives by mending. The grace of God is glue!" Which is a nice way of saying that living is the healing. Vulnerability is not a weakness. It's a strength. Very few of us are tough enough to be soft.

Much of our society doesn't work anymore, so values are much in question. We have divorce and vasectomies and work-to-rule and Hare Krishna. And we judge each other by how well we hide our emotions. We are tired of our marriages and even tired of our affairs, and our children are a burden, not so much a source of love as fear.

Once a North American grew up and married the girl next door, but today he can't remember her name, so he substitutes a quickie with a stewardess he met on a plane, and rushes off the next morning to a conference in Maine. TV producers have become the priests of our society, psychiatrists its geisha girls, and where once we loved people and used things, today it is the reverse.

We are a society of winners where almost everybody feels himself a loser, where cut of clothes and size of genitals as well as make of car tell us who we are. We are a youth cult where everyone is made to feel old, a love cult where far too many feel unloved. And because we set up life so it hurts, most of us hurt a lot.

The time has come for us to ask ourselves what we want from life, and what we have to give, and it's time for us to learn to trust and care again before it is too late.

The Greeks have a legend about a youth named Narcissus who was loved by all the nymphs including Echo, the fairest of them all. She could not tell him of her love because she could only repeat what was said to her. One day Narcissus was in the woods, and she heard him calling to his companions, "Come!"

"Come," she repeated shyly, stepping forward through the branches with her arms outstretched. But on seeing her, Narcissus ran away, saying only, "I'd rather die than give you power over me." Echo was heartbroken and as he fled, her words humbly entreating him, "I give you power over me," could be heard echoing in the woods. They were heard by one of the other nymphs, who, feeling the youth had been too cruel, uttered a prayer that he might feel what it is to love and meet no return of affection.

Thus it was that when Narcissus stopped at the pool to drink, he saw his own reflection in the water and fell in love with it. And so he spent the rest of his life seeking in vain to be loved back.

2

*Each man holds
between his hands a silence
that he wants to fill,
so he fills it with
his dreams*

Every decade dreams new dreams and throws out the
ones that went before. The fifties promised commitment while freedom went in chains. And then the
sixties came along promising freedom and personal
growth, but commitment got lost en route. It is only
now in the seventies that we are starting to wonder
if there can be freedom without commitment, if
there can be personal growth without love, and only
now in the seventies that we are starting to ask how
we can go about getting them all.

I knew a girl who had beauty and brains and talent

and grace. She was a fortunate girl in many ways. She had a husband whom she loved and a career in which she was a success. Then her husband left her for someone else, and for a time she was not herself.

She married again, though, married a man who seemed just right, and being the girl she was, before long she'd entered into his life so totally no one would ever have guessed that there'd once been someone else.

She gave up her career in order to help her husband with his, and took up parenting for the first time to mother the young daughters he brought with him. She cooked gourmet dinners every night, and even looked after his sick aunt. And then one day, almost as if she'd been thinking about it for a long while, she took a lover and began diverting much of her energy over to him.

"I suddenly realized," she told me, with eyes that didn't smile, "that I didn't have anything in my life that wasn't Jim's. His kids were my kids, his family too, even the career I worked at was his, not mine. And I knew if I ever lost him I'd have nothing left at all, nothing that wouldn't walk out the door with him!"

Perhaps it's because we are all so desperate for love that we believe if ever it comes to us we will be happy for evermore, and when it comes along we pay with the self we had for the love we want. Because there are an awful lot of relationships around in which the dependence is so great that the vulnerability is too high, and an awful lot of people bursting out of them or looking for an escape.

It's odd to think someone might take a lover not because they love their mate too little but because they love them too much instead, or that one would have as much trouble holding firm to self in a love one has, as one does when one isn't being loved back. But the problem is the same. We can only take so much vulnerability at a time, and all of us skate back and forth across that frightening line.

I guess that's why so many anesthetize their feelings with pain-killers and booze, hoping to dull their insistent throb, and still others take theirs neat and canned in violence, noise, and speed. And it's why a lot diversify, so no one can hurt too much. And why so many of us have heard ourselves say, more than once, "If you are you, and we are us, then who is it that's I?"

To meet another and hold your ground is one of the most difficult tasks in the world, and most of us alternate between various forms of non-meeting instead. We either take on the other person's thoughts and ideas, losing our own on the way, or hold the other person at arm's length in order to protect our world, and in so doing close ourselves off in some place where we remain alone.

It's not easy to live comfortably with someone else once you understand how much power you have given them just by making them the one you love. So what was love often turns to fear, and we begin to cha-cha back and forth, to do what Nena O'Neill terms "the eternal dance of domination we call love."

"Before I was married," I heard a young wife say, "I thought the joys of sharing your life were so profound that they justified every sacrifice you might have to make. But now I look at how I've changed and feel I have to put a stop to that at whatever cost."

Being in a dependent relationship is like being in a canoe—if one person needs to stretch his legs, the other is beset by vertigo. And those who set up their lives in such a way find that they either spare their partners that malaise at the expense of what they need themselves, or pay with guilt for everything they do. So many think you have to run away from love to find yourself, although that is not true.

Once there was pressure on people to marry and now there is pressure to break up, and divorce has become an obligatory rite of passage for those who want to grow. We used to look for one person to give us everything, and now many do not believe in love at all. But the walking wounded multiply, along with their defenses, so the answers can't lie there.

People give many reasons for running away from the love they have—a wish for more, a need to grow, boredom, wanting to be valued for the qualities that go unrecognized at home. But there are other reasons not as simply seen, reasons just as true. We are all afraid of love and of its hold on us, and like the alcoholic who wants one more for the road, we always feel the next one will cure us of our cowardice and the pain will go.

We have to recognize this fear and the things we do to insulate ourselves from love. And I think as well we have to learn how to *be love*, rather than to seek love, so that love can grow from us instead of being consumed.

If you think of yourself as half a couple your emotional well-being will fluctuate according to how the one person in your life is treating you, keeping you always vulnerable and self-involved. But if you think of yourself as one person, complete and total in yourself, with many sources of supply and several people nearby to love, when someone isn't giving to you, it is possible for you to give to them instead.

Couples look inward and cut off the world, and in time they use each other up. One mate, one friend, a mate expected to be friend as well—the problem is the same. A world of twosomes is a world cut off, pretty islands floating by themselves.

Instead of relationships which close us off, we need relationships which open us to ourselves, relationships which help us to be more than what we are. And above all, we need more than one. Friends are like windows through which you see out into the world and back into yourself, so they are very important to how one views one's life, and if you don't have friends you see much less than you otherwise might.

There are many who believe that fulfillment is to be found by finding one person and sharing your life with them, but I do not think that is how it works, because so many of the people who believe in that are looking for the perfect person still while other sources of fulfillment pass them by.

I think instead that life is round, that the current runs from each to each and then back a different way, and when it does not, life is a broken thing.

And I would tell you this—if you are looking for a friend, look for a person who is loved. Look for a friend with many sources of supply. And while there might be days when you'll wonder if there'll be anything left for you, in general I think that you will find what you get is a richer brew.

I don't know why it is so hard for us to understand this and to recognize that when you have a mate you need your friends more, not less. Or why we tend to fear that love will fly away if it is shared, or that what doesn't get locked in will disappear. But marriage has done terrible things to friendship in the name of love.

I knew a girl once who had a jealous husband, and a friend or two or three. And all the love that they put into her he siphoned off, saying "Me, me, me!" And when her friends needed her he begrudged them every hour, until finally they went away and left them both alone. It wasn't until then that he learned what everyone else had always known. It was not her he loved but what she got from them—the gaiety from the laughing one, the wisdom from the one with braids.

We are taught to assume that all the love that doesn't come to us goes off and away, but a lot of it just takes the long road home, and oddly enough the people we fear most often feed us, though we think they take the food from our mouths.

And maybe when I think of it, it is also true that the lover whom I once had, who took up with my confidant and friend, decided to get what I gave to him from the source instead of from the stream. And if this was the case, we can hardly blame him after all. Much of what I gave to him came to me from her.

3

If you can't commit to something big, commit to something small

I know a man who has searched for fulfillment all his life. In the beginning, perhaps because he was born poor, he thought it had to do with having the things that money seems to carry in its wake. And after he'd become an engineer and then a developer and a millionaire, he discovered that money was not it. He tried women, and fancy cars, and even a dog and a yacht, but they failed him too. So he tried traveling, and not working, and ultimately dropping out. But nothing seemed to work.

By the time I'd met him he'd searched everywhere anyone could suggest he look, searched and searched, trying to find he knew not what. He tried guitar lessons, taking three a day, one in classical guitar, one in flamenco, and one from a hippie folk-singer who taught him also about grass. He tried figure skating, practicing every afternoon between four and six, working his figures out with his slide rule in a three-ring binder every night. He tried antique collecting, filling his apartment up with so many grandfather clocks and Persian rugs he had to open a store. He alternately tried eating and dieting and getting married and getting divorced, and finally he tried fasting and celibacy and giving up his worldly goods.

He'd been a Buddhist monk for several years when I saw him next. His hair was gray, he wore a robe, but he still looked the same. And when I asked him if he'd found fulfillment yet, he answered, "No, it's out there still."

No one knows much about fulfillment except that it's hard to find, and maybe doesn't exist, and a lot of people who believe in it when they are twenty stop believing in it later on. You can look too hard for fulfillment, and you can not look hard enough. And although you're guaranteed the right to pursue it, it isn't a money-back guarantee, so there is no one to complain to if you blow it and spend your life barking up the wrong tree.

Fulfillment is always something the other guy's

got, something just over the hill. It's an immensely agile boxer who lets us get him in a clinch a hundred times a day but then somehow slips away. It's the pot of gold at the end of the rainbow, and catching the brass ring. It's true love, becoming rich, and even staying thin. But whatever it is, it always eludes you and keeps you on the run like the carrot on the stick, and even when it bites your line a million times you rarely reel it in.

All of us feel there must be more, but wonder what the more really is, and often the more we yearned for last year isn't enough today. So we wait in vain for something else, something just a little better than what we've got, and often we trade in the thing we have for something we think we should want.

We are the "Is this all there is?" generation, waiting for the perfect thing to commit to—the perfect job, the perfect love—and we feel miserable all the while we wait, somehow failing to understand that loneliness lies in the suspended state.

Some feel the lack of fulfillment our generation feels stems from our unwillingness to commit. We live at a time when modern communications make us aware of so many things we can do nothing about, and tell us of the suffering of countless people we have no choice but to try and shut out. So a lot of us have stopped caring or, caring so much that we feel impotent and frail, have had to reduce our pain by pretending the suffering of people we don't know is somehow not quite real.

And there is another problem modern communications bring—the dream of perfection fostered by a host of adman's dreams. We live ringed around by sugar-plum fairies, dancing at us from every page and every screen, and real life when we meet it never seems somehow as good. We are encouraged to expect perfection, and perfection doesn't exist, so we are always a little disappointed and hold back again, hoping the next round will really be it.

It's nice to have choices, and flexibility makes life more interesting, it's true, but you can get lost on the sea of infinite possibilities, and there is nothing liberating about that. And people who are always trying to make the perfect choice, rejecting what they have for what they hope to find, bet the present on the future and end up missing both.

The Greeks had a legend about a man named Sisyphus who was banished by Zeus to a desert island, an island which had nothing on it to keep him occupied. And after a while Sisyphus started losing his mind. Then one day he took it into his head to push a big rock up the mountain on the island, and all day long he labored with the big rock, pushing it and pushing it in the hot sun, until at night, with the top of the hill almost in sight, he finally gave up and let the rock roll down the hill again. He did this again the next day, and the next, and for many months to come, and though he never reached the top of the mountain with his rock, when they finally found him he was sane, just as sane as he'd ever been.

I've always liked this story because it made me conscious of something which I'd only half guessed before—the fact that it's our commitment to life which saves us, and what we commit to is not what's important at all. I know it's not easy to rid yourself of the notion that you need something important to commit to, or to learn to find pleasure in what is, rather than displeasure in what you wish there'd be, but the trick of life is to stop worrying about finding the perfect something to commit to and commit to something, anything at all. And if you can't commit to something big, then commit to something small.

4

So that love can grow from you

I knew a young man a long time ago from a faraway place who met an American girl on a boat going to Europe when he was in his teens, and he fell in love with her and she with him. It was a star-crossed romance in many ways, but especially so because they were of different religions, and the young man, having been very strictly brought up, considered his feelings for the girl taboo. As soon as the ship docked in Le Havre he went immediately to confession, hoping a good father at the church could tell him what to do. And the priest he found there advised him to give up this girl, warning him that such a match had too many obstacles. And so he returned to the boat with his mind made up, although he said nothing to the girl and, grievously distressed, vowed not to see her again.

This was not easy to do because the tour he was on arrived in many places on the same day as her tour did, and many of his schoolmates had made friends with schoolmates of hers and planned to spend time together along the way. He spent the whole day at Versailles trying to avoid her in the garden while she looked everywhere for him, breaking his heart. And when they arrived in Florence and all his companions rushed over to the pension where she was staying to take her friends for gelati, he went to bed early, claiming he was sick, although he didn't want to and regretted it all evening long.

He didn't see her again until his boat train docked in North America at the end of his tour. And then, when he saw her there with her friends at the station and heard them invite him and his tour mates back to her house for lunch, he knew he was caught and went along willingly, although he was horrified to realize he still felt as strongly about her as he ever did. But after the lunch was over, his heart was beating so wildly that he knew there was no hope for him if he remained in her presence any longer, so he went to the airport and took the first plane home, leaving his trunk for his friends to deal with, and her wondering where he'd gone.

A year later to the day, he wrote her a letter explaining everything, and five years later he came back, resolved to marry her at whatever cost. But it was too late. He arrived to find she'd just married someone else, and he went quietly away once more. He didn't see her again for close to twenty years and by the time he did he was married himself, although not very happily, and had three children, two boys and a girl. And then one day one of his former schoolmates came back from a business trip to North America and told him he had seen her and that she was now divorced.

He had to find her, he knew that. He'd run away from her once, fearing to love her and fearing loving would cost him himself, but now he knew the consequences of not loving were worse. And he understood that running away had been a mistake, and that he wanted very much to see her, and to see if he could pick up where he left off.

It took him six trips to North America before he found her and he had to call the police station and all the people listed under her former husband's name in a city of two million before he tracked her down. And after he had talked with her and after they had laughed and cried till dawn, he knew it wasn't her he'd run away from so long ago, but a deep fear inside himself, a fear of commitment maybe, a fear of caring too much. And he knew that what she represented wasn't so much the foreign other as the unexplored side of himself.

It is easy to spend your life looking for an elusive something, always holding out for what you don't quite know, and many of us do it, without recognizing that we are looking for ourselves. The search for the perfect other is always a search for what we sense we lack. And the reason that we never find them is because the search goes on as long as we feel inadequate ourselves.

There is no perfect person who can make you whole. You have to do that yourself, and if you wait for someone to fill you up you always wait in vain, because no one is ever equal to the task. Waiting for another to give to you always makes you feel vulnerable and insecure. The only way you ever feel strong and sure is when you are giving to others instead of wishing that they would give to you.

It is very hard to learn that lesson and to stop hoping to get from others what you must provide yourself. And it is even harder still to stop waiting for someone to give to you, and to start looking instead for what you might have that you can give to someone else. But giving is the key.

I remember once trying to comfort a friend who

was depressed, but weeks went by and she showed no signs of waking back to life. And then one day all of a sudden she called me up and there was laughter in her voice, and when I asked her what had brought about the change she said she'd found a friend who was worse off than she and trying to help him had cured her of herself.

I like to think of life as a bank in which emotional currency gets put in and drawn out. And sometimes you get out of the bank what you put in, and sometimes you get back some other thing, and the energy you put in is passed on to someone else. And while sometimes those who make the largest deposits don't draw out as much as some who deposit less, energy invested pays a dividend nonetheless. And while I know there are those who will say the question of who gives and who takes, who deposits and who withdraws, is settled in the cradle or even in the womb, and who the squanderers will be and who will husband what they have and keep it for themselves, whether energy or goods, is all predetermined and not likely to be changed, I just thought I'd mention that the gift I'm talking about here is not to another person, it is to yourself.

When I was a little girl our class helped a family every Christmas, and sometimes they were grateful and sometimes they were not. Then one year when we reached our destination with our presents and found another grade had arrived before us, a boy in our class asked why we should help a family anyway. "What have they ever done for us?" And the teacher asked each of us to describe how we felt when we were gathering up clothes and food to take to them, and when he had a collection of "greats" and "helpfuls" and "kinds" he said, "That's what the family did for you. You gave them turkey and they gave you those warm feelings back."

Perhaps the biggest source of unhappiness in the world today stems from the idea that there is someone out there who will meet all our needs, because it turns us into needful children, waiting to be fed, instead of healthy adults asking if there is anyone who might need us. We are not vessels in need of filling up, we are persons in our own right with resources of our own.

There is an ancient Iranian allegory written in the thirteenth century by Farid ud-din Attar about the Simurgh, an immortal bird who makes his nest in the branches at the top of the tree of knowledge. One day one of the Simurgh's silver feathers is found in the middle of China, and the other birds, tired of being without a leader, decide to seek him out so that he can give their lives some direction. They know only that his name means "thirty birds" and that he makes his castle in the Kaf, the range of mountains that rings the earth.

At the outset some of the birds lose heart and claim they cannot make the trip. The nightingale pleads his love for the rose, the parrot pleads his beauty for which he lives caged. The partridge cannot leave his home in the hills, the heron his home in the marshes, the owl his ruins. But finally a delegation of birds sets out on this perilous venture. They travel for many days and years and cross through seven valleys and seas, the last two bearing the names Bewilderment and Annihilation. Many of the pilgrims desert, and the journey takes its toll among the rest. Finally thirty birds made pure by their suffering reach the great peak of the Simurgh. At last they behold him, and they realize that they are the Simurgh, and that the Simurgh is each and all of them.

Part Two
CONNECTING

I know you have nothing.
That is why I ask you for everything.
That way you will have everything.
ANTONIO PORCHIA

5

Some of our defenses are more primitive than others

There is a sixth-century Indian legend about a scorpion and a tortoise who were facing a swollen river, and the scorpion begged the tortoise to carry him across. "I can't take you on my back," the tortoise replied. "You'd sting me."

"Why would I do that?" the scorpion wanted to know. "You'd be my life raft. If I stung you we'd both drown."

"Well," said the tortoise, "since you put it that way, I guess it'll be all right. Hop on."

So the scorpion climbed on the tortoise's back and they set out across the river and when they were almost to the shore, the scorpion stung the tortoise, and as they were both going down, the tortoise turned to the scorpion and asked, "Just tell me this, before we drown. Why did you do it? I have to know."

And the scorpion replied, looking perhaps a little regretful, "What can I tell you? I couldn't help myself. It's my nature."

There are people who yell, and those who are shy. There are ones who resent, and ones who hide. There are those who joke and those who act, and lots who compete with everyone in sight. There are some who patronize and some who collapse, and some who capture and some who buy.

There is a beast in all of us which protects us from the world, and while in some of us it is a roaring beast and in others it is a beast that crawls, we all have defenses that we use more than we need, and for everything they protect us from they cost us something more. Defenses come in many forms, many more than I can name, and while some of them are more primitive than others, they all keep the world away from us just the same.

I am not sure why we all feel so vulnerable or why so many of us go through life like wounded beasts, crouched and waiting for the other guy to strike, but almost everyone sees himself as a loser down deep inside and fails to understand that others are frightened too. And a lot of people lash out first, fearing they will be hurt if they don't, and much of our social behavior has to do with throwing others off our trail before they find us out.

I suppose closing yourself off from your feelings frees you, at a price, from having to do anything about them. And putting other people in parentheses, or dancing away yourself, very often seems a safer bet than taking your chances on their behavior once you've let them in. But you must keep in mind that if you are defending all the time, you are pushing away life, and the life you are pushing away is your own.

I don't think we always know just how it is we push intimacy away, or how deep and wide we've dug our moat. There are so many masks to hide behind, so many ways to get lost inside, that it's very easy to lock yourself away and lose the capacity to get out alive.

I knew a man once who owned a Renoir, a small perfect portrait of a young girl wearing a blue bonnet, and when he had guests he paraded them slowly around his living room showing them his various objets d'art, stopping finally in front of the Renoir for them to admire his best piece. And after the tour there was usually a brandy before the baronial fireplace, with its tiger skin, and a lecture on the money to be made from buying art, during which the host invariably mentioned all the money he had made himself.

I watched this show-and-tell routine several times before I asked the man who owned the portrait of the young girl if he bought the painting because he loved it or because he viewed it as a good investment, making it clear that I meant no offense with this question and understood that to everything there is an art. But he looked at me for a long time after I asked the question, shaking his head as if disappointed in me, and then finally he said, "I didn't buy it for either of those reasons. I thought you could see. I bought it for a show-off, and it's done the job magnificently."

There was a magazine article some time ago in which an anthropologist described a primitive tribe somewhere who wore their portraits on their foreheads and bowed to each other's picture, paying their obeisance to the image rather than to the owner underneath. And I remember thinking when I read about that tribe how much like them we were, although we think ourselves civilized and them simple beyond words.

Perhaps it is because we try so hard to show others how bright we are, how generous or how rich, that we never see we're making them work twice as hard to feel good about themselves. And people who are busy defending themselves rarely ask if the defenses they are using cause others to like them more or less, and they almost never notice how frightened the other person is of them.

There was a girl I went to school with who'd been trained by tough-minded nuns to do her very best at all times, and to do it better than anyone else. She worked very hard, studied all the time, had her hand permanently on the rise, but no one ever liked her. They don't like her still, and they never gave her the approval her good behavior should have won. I don't think she ever realized that the more she tried, the further behind she fell, or that while she was showing everyone how much she knew, the message they were getting was that she thought herself better than she considered them.

I had a friend once whose approval I sought, and so I tried each time I saw her to impress her with what I could do, but the harder I tried the less inclined she was to smile on me. And though I tried even harder and then harder still again, I never got her approval. I got rejections by the gross. It took me years to realize what was happening between her and me and to think of giving her my approval instead of asking for hers, and by the time I finally figured this out, it was too late for us.

I still feel badly when I think of how I broke down her door with my requests and am embarrassed when I recollect that it never dawned on me that others have needs as great as mine. We're all so self-involved, expecting others to feed us first and never asking who is feeding them, always ready with the excuse that we are shy or we are hurt.

Life is very much like an arms race, each side waiting for the other one to put his stick down first, and just carrying a stick, any kind of stick, is likely to get you a rap on the head. "In any fighting group," Camus wrote not so long ago, "one needs men who kill and men who cure. I have chosen to cure, but I still know I am fighting." And I think this is precisely what we have to decide ourselves. We have to know if we are fighting for life or against it, and if we want to shut it out or let it in. Only then can we decide which weapons to use.

If I had to say which defenses guard you best through life, I'd say there are no good ones at all, and that you are most safe when you put down your weapons, and your fears, and worry instead about how to make the other person feel comfortable about you.

I know there are people you should not touch, but must stand back and let them touch you instead, and people to whom you must be the first to hold out a hand, and it's sometimes hard to know which is which. But learning how to make others trust you is the best protection there is. And it will make you safer than all the armor you can find.

6

Push-pull, click-click

I overheard a young man once saying to his wife, "I can't control you. That's the problem and it's been the problem ever since day one!" And then I heard her answer him and heard her terrible voice. "No!" she said. "The problem isn't that you can't control me, the problem is you're trying to. Why don't you stop worrying about controlling me and start worrying about controlling yourself?"

A lot of people make their lives more complicated than they need to be by trying to control others who don't want their help, struggling in vain to win battles they could win more easily just by keeping out. And many people who wouldn't dream of trying to control a friend spend more time than they should trying to manage their spouse.

There are people who try to dominate others out of fear, and there are people who do it for the fun of being the one with clout. And there are many who do it not knowing what they do, or because they've always done it and know no other way.

I knew a man sometime back who liked to send presents to the ladies he fancied. Right after he met them he would send them long-stemmed roses. Then if they accepted his invitation to lunch he would send them a little memento of the afternoon. As the relationships progressed, more and more presents would arrive—silver bracelets, crystal decanters, negligees with marabou trim. Usually by the time he asked for something in return, the girl he'd been courting was so indebted she couldn't possibly say no. So he got what he wanted, although occasionally one of them balked, and when she did he would always complain that there was no gratitude anymore.

From time to time a girl would outsmart him and, recognizing that he was not really giving but buying and selling, she would keep him on the hook a little longer, indicating with a saucy wave of her head that the price wasn't quite right. And he would always throw in another present or two, maybe a Patek Philippe watch or a weekend in Paris.

When giving is used as a way of controlling others, the giver is really asking for something for himself.

A lot of people thought it was sex this man was after, but that's too simple. It was power he wanted, because if he had only wanted sex he wouldn't have put a price on it.

When he bought his companion he got more than sex—he got to feel superior to her. And by confirming for himself that everyone has a price, he felt powerful. All he needed was money and he could have anything he wanted. In short, he was playing a variation of the old joke, "Would you sleep with me for a million dollars? You would? Great! Now that that's established, we can haggle over the price."

Push-pull, click-click. Insist upon being the giver and you reduce the other person one step from a beggar. And if you want to diminish them still further you can simply promise and not deliver, thereby keeping them always waiting, always thanking, always not quite sure. Or you can get others to dance and sing songs for you, promising to reward them for a job well done, and then not ever be quite satisfied with them.

A young university lecturer whom I knew when I went to school told me of a problem that he had at work. And as the story began to unfold it became clear that the man who he thought was championing his cause was really the problem and that without him it wouldn't exist. The young man was up for promotion, which meant he would pass out of the older man's control, so the older man invented a problem that only he could solve. He told the young man how much opposition there was to his appointment, how many people there were who didn't want him around. And then when the young man was appointed, the older man took a lot of bows for managing the impossible and getting the appointment through anyhow. And the young man felt grateful as well as dependent, so the older professor didn't have to worry about losing his control over him for a while.

Getting control over others has a lot to do with making them feel weak. You can make them feel indebted or make them feel inadequate in yet some other way. Just as the wife of an impotent husband can keep him permanently out of commission simply by saying, "I can't believe you've managed an erection!" whenever there is any sign of a change, so all the ways that increase another's dependence on you and give you control are a mixed blessing which have a hidden price. And many a person who kept another from growing up and away then found they had to carry that person for the rest of their days.

I knew a couple years ago, and you've likely met them too, who were awkward to be with because of the husband's habit of ordering his wife around, barking orders at her like the captain of a ship, and the wife's habit of scurrying about, carrying out his bidding as if she were a maid. Everyone who knew this couple felt sorry for the wife and wanted to protect her from her spouse, and then one day after she'd left him, it became clear he hadn't been her captor, it was he who'd been the slave.

There are many ways of controlling other people. You can overpower them or underpower yourself. You can take them by force or take them by surprise. You can go through life saying poor me or play the little lost child. Weakness is a kind of strategy. The victory isn't always to the strong. The weak have their weapons too. They come and collapse on you like defeated nations and you have to look after them. There are an awful lot of people who would rather be pitied than feel fulfilled.

When you let another person control you, you put them in charge and then whatever happens to you afterwards is their affair. Which means they not only have to do all the work but also take the blame. And if you want to break out at any time you can always say you had to leave because you were pushed around, so you sidestep responsibility even then.

Power breeds resentment and withers the slow-growing plant that is trust, and people who use it to capture others not only fail to make friends but often end up captives themselves. And perhaps what is sadder still is that when you control other people you take away all that there might be in a real encounter with them and replace it with your fears. And while you might get gratitude for a while, or guilt and tears, you won't get what they had to offer if you'd let them give you what was really in their hearts.

7

If I am not for myself, who will be for me?

There used to be an artist living near me who was in love with a married woman, and every day after her husband went to work she came to visit her lover in his studio and spend the day with him. The artist loved her very much and she loved him as well, but he could never forget the fact that she was not his alone, and he tormented himself with thoughts of her with other men. He told his friends about his fears and how they kept him up at night and said he could not help thinking that she might have other loves as well as him. And while his friends laughed at him at first and assured him that he had the best of life—a lover who stayed all day and left you wanting more—in time they recognized his pain and thought of ways to help him out.

"I'll try to seduce her," one of them said. "We'll put your fears to bed, and if she isn't true you'll soon know the worst." And the artist agreed and thanked him for his help. No one knows what happened after that, at least no one knows for sure, but not long afterward the artist died from a bullet wound to the head. And there seems little doubt that he died by his own hand, although he left no note.

I've thought about him a lot over the years, and wished he hadn't died, and every time I think of him the thought that comes to mind is that we are all a little like him in that we often fear being rejected so very much that we reject ourselves first before anyone else has the chance.

Most of us doubt ourselves now and then, and some of us doubt ourselves quite a lot, and many a relationship that didn't have to end was brought to convulsion by someone who was afraid. Almost all the games we play with others have at the bottom of them the real confrontation with ourselves, and when you doubt yourself you doubt everyone else as well. So what is thought to be fear of others often is really distrust of self, just as what is usually seen as narcissism or self-love is more often the inability to love, caused by a big dose of self-hate.

I've always wondered why some people don't seem to have to wait for others to accept them but accept themselves first, while others—no matter how much love they get—stand begging forever at a door they themselves have closed.

It is thought that believing in yourself has a lot to do with how you've been raised, and certainly some who like themselves don't have half as much to like as those who don't like themselves at all. So no doubt it's true that when you are raised by approving parents you are more believing in yourself. But it's no easy matter to accept yourself, or to be the person that you are, and an awful lot of us wait for others to define us or to give us permission to be what we've always been.

We are all persons courtesy of someone else, and since we need others to perceive us in order to experience ourselves, it is very hard to like yourself when those nearest you seem to doubt your worth. And when those around you don't see you as you want to see yourself, it is only too easy to lose the way and start auditioning instead for them.

"If you can't be yourself," Tennessee Williams wrote, "what's the point of being anyone else?" And most of us would agree, but it's harder than it sounds. There are so many masks we are expected to wear to cover our real face that some people don't always know themselves when they see themselves naked in the glass. And a lot of people never find themselves to like.

We are all connected to the world by a thousand hidden strings that we don't see. There are the strings of other people's expectations and those we make ourselves out of vanity or fear. And the world is very quick to hang a myth on you which can cover you like a net, and if you aren't nimble enough to jump clear of it you can spend your life inside.

A colleague of mine once described a man we both knew as being "a very proud man who had lost his opinion of himself and had hence to slink away," and it still makes me smile to think of how well he put the problem trying to be something that you are not creates. It is too bad so many people make the mistake of thinking pride will win them the respect they want, when it's humility they really need.

Some people feel accepting yourself means being proud, but to me being proud means being insecure. When you are really proud you don't need to put on false airs. You simply accept yourself as you are and expect others will do the same.

I know there are those who feel vanity did more

for civilization than honesty will ever do, but it seems to me that it is better to have compassion for yourself, and come to terms with who you are, than it is to spend your life trying to please the crowd. When you look to other people to approve of you instead of approving of yourself, you make them the judge of your worth and give them power over you, but they haven't got that power unless you consign it to them yourself.

So if you must seek approval, choose the right audience to seek it from, and if you don't like what you hear get another opinion, get two or three. And when someone wants you to be what you aren't or refuses you permission to be who you are, try to understand that that is their problem, really, and you don't have to make it yours. And don't let anyone tell you you have to be perfect to be loved, because that simply isn't true. If the people in your life only love you if you put on a false front, they don't love you after all, so you haven't much to lose.

There are psychologists who feel the amount of self-disclosure we are capable of says a good deal about the state of our mental health. And they point out that those who are the most open with others are those who have the closest friends.

And they also say one of the reasons women live longer than men in our society is that they are allowed to be more honest about themselves and hence have less to hide.

Pride and dignity are just more acceptable forms of hubris after all, but they are hubris nevertheless, and they can wall you in. When you pretend to be somebody other than the person you are, your estrangement from yourself keeps others away from you as well. And in time alienation becomes a way of life.

We show whom we love by whom we trust with our real selves. And when we put up a false front, we are saying to those we meet, "I don't trust you, which is why I don't show you my true face." And while very often the reason we don't let others see us as we see ourselves is not that we don't like them but that we don't love ourselves, the message we send out is that it's them we can't abide.

Some people let others define them because they need their approval so much they are willing to let them call the shots, and others do it because they are so lacking in self-worth they are afraid that if anyone found out who they really were they would be rejected out of hand. But if being honest means that occasionally you give yourself away by acknowledging limitations in yourself that someone might have missed before, well, that's only as bad as you consider it to be.

We are all constantly remodeling ourselves, trying for a better fit between the inner imperatives and the outer demands, and like the blind man exploring the elephant we go through life with only the smallest bit in hand, judging the whole by the little we know. It is important to bear this in mind, and to keep in mind as well that we are judged not by what we know but by the honesty of our search.

"Man staggers through life, yapped at by his reason, pulled and shoved by his appetites, whispered to by his fears, and beckoned to by his hopes," Eric Hoffer wrote, and he was right. We can each of us only do our best. Life is after all a search for the secrets of growth and nobody is expected to have them all.

8

Very few of us are tough enough to be soft

A man told me recently that his uncle had jumped off a building in Tel Aviv while his family sat assembled on the terrace taking tea. The uncle was an exceptional man, a man who'd lived an extraordinary life, and while I hardly knew him, news of his death took me by surprise and made me pause to think.

He'd been born in Poland some seventy-odd years before, Jewish and unafraid, and he'd escaped death in the concentration camps because he was so smart and tough. And after the war ended, although not a young man then, he went to Palestine to fight with the Haganah, rising to the rank of major by the time he retired. He stayed on in Israel once it became a state, helping to start new industries and to till the land. And though in time he became quite rich and sent his children to schools in Paris and London and New York, he went on working and fighting in Israel, until one day a company he'd started for his son went bankrupt, and that's the day he took his life.

There is something terrifying about learning that someone you'd always felt to be much more courageous than yourself has given up the fight, and I'm not sure if the shiver we feel when we get that kind of news comes from the knowledge that we now have to push on all alone or the fear that perhaps they knew something we have yet to learn.

I've thought a lot about that man and wondered why someone like him would want to end his life, and finally, needing to know and finding the answer not in me, I went back to his nephew and asked him if he had any clues. "The answer is simple," was all he said. "He lost his self-esteem."

It seems so odd that a person who could walk calmly into a flaming house or defy a firing squad might buckle at a cocktail party, if someone calls them a bad name, or be intimidated by a clerk. But we are all spooked by different things, and fear of loss and fear of the unknown and fear of losing face are just as terrifying to many as fear of pain or death.

We all live with doubts, even the very brave, and we have our breaking point and lose our nerve from time to time, but when I thought about what the nephew said, I knew that he was right. It is much easier to be courageous when people are applauding you than when you are in defeat. And many of us who pass as brave when the crowd is all waving hats would crumble if they turned on us and starting throwing rocks.

The story of the man who chose to die rather than face disgrace stayed in my mind a long, long time, longer than I meant it to because I recognized myself in him. Life takes a lot of courage, often more than we think we've got, and almost always more than we think we should have to find. But it needn't be that tough. There are so many battles one has to face with others and with oneself, and sometimes you find you are braver than you think and sometimes you find you aren't, and one never really knows when fear and and doubt will hit. But when I think of that man who chose to die, what is most clear is that as long as we let others tell us if we rate, not one of us is safe.

There is a Buddhist fable written over 2,000 years ago by the Buddha himself, some say, about a beautiful young elephant who lived in the forest near Benares. She was as white as crane's down, according to the legend, and her size and strength were so great that the men who captured her gave her as a present to the king.

The king entrusted her to his elephant trainers to be taught to stand firm and to follow commands, but the trainers were harsh with her and beat her with their elephant goads, and one day, maddened by pain, she broke free of them and escaped.

She ran as fast as she could for many days, traveling as far into the Himalayan mountains as she could go, until she outdistanced all the king's men who were chasing her, and in time they all went home and she was free. But still she raced on, and although time passed she did not reduce her pace or forget for a moment that she had been a captive once. Every time a twig snapped or a breath of wind rustled the trees she dashed off at full speed, thrashing her trunk wildly from side to side.

Finally a compassionate tree sprite could stand her

pain no longer and leaned out of a fork in a tree one day and whispered into the elephant's ear. "Do you fear the wind? It only moves the clouds and dries the dew. You ought to look into your mind. It's fear that has captured you." And the minute the wood sprite had spoken the beautiful elephant realized that she had nothing to fear but the habit of being afraid, and she began to enjoy life again.

There are really only two ways to approach life—as victim or as gallant fighter—and you must decide if you want to act or react, deal your own cards or play with a stacked deck. And if you don't decide which way to play with life, it always plays with you.

A lot of people forget that, so they scan the books that tell you how to make people respond as you'd have them do, or look for someone to protect them from the world, but the fact is that nothing works but to learn to trust yourself, and to understand that each encounter makes you stronger, even the ones you lose.

A girl I know has been married since she was very young to a man she has loved since she was a child, and she has a life that in almost every way is story-book perfect and unblemished by hurt of any kind.

But she isn't half as strong within herself as other friends of mine who have had some bad days mixed in with the good. And although I have heard others say they envy her and that they wish their lives had been so blessed, the fact is that she is very insecure at times, and as the years go by she worries more and more about how she would survive if her husband wasn't by her side.

Courage expands with use. It isn't something you can put upon the shelf and keep in stock against a rainy day. If you don't use it, it atrophies with neglect. But it is also true that we are stronger than we think.

A man once told me about two sisters whom he knew very well because he was in love with the beautiful one and had tried unsuccessfully to win her over the span of several years. "Marilyn had a sister who always envied her," he said, choosing his words with care, "and thought of herself as second best. After all, Marilyn's beauty provided her with opportunities the sister never had." And when I pressed him to explain what kind of opportunities he meant, he answered with an ironic smile, "Well, Marilyn has had the opportunity to be carried off by an infinite number of con men, and the sister, having none, married a nice accountant who loves her to this day."

I remember how surprised I was when he ended his story that way, surprised and a little startled to realize that it wasn't the pretty one who held all the cards, but the one who didn't know she did. So few of us really recognize what our assets are, or even what they are not, and too often we want what we haven't got, and fail to see what we have. And many of us impoverish our lives by failing to recognize that our resources are greater than we think.

It can be very hard to find the courage to face life wholeheartedly and to respond honestly, knowing that there are no guarantees. And many of us are afraid to fully experience the other person, and to hear with an open heart what is being said to us, and to speak our own truth back no matter what reception we think we'll get.

And sometimes when we've been in the habit of not taking any chances for a long time—of hedging our bets even when someone is reaching out to us— it seems too hard to reach back to them, too much to demand of ourselves. So we give up before we try to discover whether there is something out there to meet, and sit back instead to complain about life, because we haven't got the courage to move out beyond ourselves.

It's hard to know how to be a better friend, more responsive, more open, more aware. And even harder to know how to dip inside yourself to where you hide love and to find it so you have enough to feed yourself and to give it away besides. But I do know this—the people who do it best aren't people who wait for others to validate them, they validate themselves. And when the moment comes when everyone waits, the moment when each person hopes the other will make the first move, they don't say, "I wish I was better looking or had more money in the bank." They just extend a hand and smile. That's usually all it takes.

Part Three

TOUCHING

*You will find the distance
that separates you from them,
by joining them.*
ANTONIO PORCHIA

The gift that goes on giving

Being emotionally there for other people involves listening with your whole self to everything they are saying, and to what they aren't saying besides. And if you really do this well you will hear what they are hoping, and what they are fearing, and what they can't acknowledge even to themselves. And you will be able to live with them in their world and to share what they feel inside.

Many people only hear the words that are said, and then wonder why they never quite understand what is happening in their lives, forgetting that words don't tell it all—there are also the spaces in between, and the eyes and the hands. And there is what is said by reason, and what is said at a level where the intellect doesn't dwell.

You can't just listen to the people whom you love with your ears, you have to listen as well with your heart, and to recognize that there are several of them talking to you although you might see only one. Sometimes the rational self sends signals which the emotional self contradicts, and frequently the whole truth isn't told by either one.

Often we pick up messages people are sending us unconsciously but, not quite wanting to acknowledge them or considering them too dangerous to take out and examine in the light, we let them pass by us, only to find they reappear as dreams—memories we tried to forget, fantasies we couldn't quite face, twinges of embarrassment and pain. These are messages missed by the intellect, signals from our subconscious hoping for another chance to make their point.

We are big on the rational in the western world, mistrusting the emotions except when they tell us something we can measure and count. And too often we forget as well that the body can teach us things that aren't in any of the books, and that the heart knows things that reason can't understand.

The older I get the less store I put by what is thought, and the more I try to listen for what is written on the wind. I don't know why we often think the rational is all we need. It is at best a stratification of what we know intuitively, and then we often get it wrong trying to fit what we just learned to what we learned last week.

Poets talk of "having lines land on them" and claim that what they write is hanging in the air for anyone to reach. When someone asked William Blake where he got his ideas, he said that he stuck his finger through the floor of heaven and pulled them down. And Michaelangelo turned away the congratulations someone proffered him on turning a block of stone into a man, claiming the man was in there all the time and just required a little help in getting out.

It's true that some people have larger gifts for seeing what there is, and some can't see what is in front of their nose, while others can see through a brick wall. But all of us have had the experience of knowing something in the morning that we didn't know the night before, and I think that is because when we open up we can receive much better and so what is out there to be known finds its way to us.

The more aware we are the better we can respond. And we will react not just to the way the other person is treating us, or to what they have to say, but to them, and to that which is inside them which calls out even when they do not know they do.

Really responding to another person means accepting what they feel, not making judgments, not censoring, and not asking that they just tell you things you might like to hear. If you demand that they only have solvable problems or speak only of things that amuse, you are denying their reality and leaving them alone.

It is easy to make the mistake of assuming that the person talking to us wants our advice. And too often we rush to tell other people what we think or what they ought to do, when what they really want from us as a friend is just that we hear and be with them to give them strength.

It is hard to listen to other people and hear what they are really saying, and not to use your power over them or make a convenience of them. And a lot of people get confused when they listen to a friend about what the purpose of that listening is, and feel they should do something to help out. So they either take their friend's life away from them or, trying so hard to pull them from the hole they're in, fall inside themselves.

The job of a friend is not to decide what should be done, not to run interference or pick up the slack. The job of a friend is to understand, and to supply energy and hope, and in doing so to keep those they value on their feet a little longer, so that they can fight another round and grow stronger in themselves.

$\mathcal{S}$ome people listen willingly, but in responding always seem to appear above it all somehow, as if the situation they are hearing about could never have happened to them. Perhaps it is that they have led too orderly a life, or maybe they offer sympathy when it is empathy that is needed. There is a difference between sympathy and empathy, and the difference is that sympathy always has an edge, a hint that the person offering it feels superior and smug, while when you are empathetic, the person you are responding to knows you feel for them, and that you understand that you could but for the grace of God go there as well.

There isn't one of us who might not have been destroyed by events at some time in the past, or might not be destroyed still if the gods were to conspire against us, and send us trouble but no friend. So we must not forget that the word "respond" comes from the same root as does "responsibility," or that the friend whom you save today will be that much stronger when the tomorrow comes that you have to call on them.

We live in a society in which psychiatrists sell

friendship by the hour, and people who want for friends pay to lie upon the couch. The time has come for us to learn how to hold each other's hand instead, and how to care for each other in ways that really work. Some say loneliness is a condition of the soul, but I think it is a yearning to be understood—and that means when we are bad as well as when we're good. There are always people to love you when you are a success, but fewer to listen to you when you're in distress, and we all need friends who are there in our less than perfect times, as good friends in our pain as in our joy.

Friendship is the gift that goes on giving and is a gift to both the person given to and to the giver as well. But to really make it work it isn't enough to give to another person, you have also to let them give to you.

I met a family a summer or two ago that had four children, one of whom had a musical talent that was special and rare. The mother—there was no father, he had departed some time before—scraped and sacrificed to see that this special son got the kind of education that his talent deserved. And when the uniforms and pocket money for his school supplies came to more than she could provide, the other children willingly put their dreams aside.

The musical son was a thin, sensitive boy who didn't seem meant for hard work, and to add to his delicate nature he had an impractical streak. Once when he'd picked fruit a whole summer side by side with his brothers and sisters to help buy their clothes for the next year, he passed the offices of the Society for Crippled Children on the way home and gave his whole paycheck to the man behind the desk.

He'd been in the musical college almost two years when word came back that he'd quit. He'd been lying on his bed all day anyway, he told his mother, shutting the door first thing in the morning and not letting anyone in. His mother was heartbroken and so, to a lesser degree, were his brothers and sister, and they still wonder why he threw away his one big chance. They blamed his weak nature, and his delicate health, and the fact that he didn't appreciate how hard the real world is. And when he made the decision to be a missionary and go off, as he put it, "to help those less fortunate than myself," they didn't understand at all.

It can be much harder to be on the receiving end of a transaction than to be the one who gets to give. In fact, being given to can mean being taken from. There is a very strong connection between pride and giving, and those who do the giving get to feel that they are worthy, while those who are given to often feel that they are not.

I once had a boyfriend who exited from my house one evening shouting back at me, "You are more loving than I, more generous, and more forgiving!" Then he slammed the door, never to return. I remember yelling after him, "Have you got any other complaints?" but he taught me a lot.

Nobody will thank you for pointing out to them that they aren't as giving as you, or even as giving as they wish they were. So you have to be very careful when you give to others that you don't tell them how great you are rather than how much you value them.

It's hard to know whether to give sometimes. I find I have to look deeper into my own motives for giving than I used to. You know the definition of a sadist—someone who is nice to a masochist. Well, giving is a very complicated business, and it is important to ask yourself how the person on the receiving end is likely to feel about your gift before you make it.

I had a friend once whose good fortune wasn't equal to mine, and so I tried to share my luck with her. But whatever I did in whatever way, she spurned my gifts and me. And after a while it became quite clear that there was no way that I could do anything for her because she wouldn't let me, and so I went away feeling sad and not quite sure. And it was a long time before I began to see that I was taking away from her with my gifts, not giving to her at all.

We are all guilty from time to time of giving in a way which pleases us at the expense of someone else. Perhaps we know someone who isn't earning very much money, so we always overpower them when it comes time to pay the bill. One could argue that we are just being thoughtful, but it is just as likely that we are really saying, "I've got my life together and you have not." Or maybe we have a friend whose taste in clothes is so terrible we volunteer to lend her ours every time she has an important date, convincing her that we are certain she'd never make it without our help.

Giving is only giving if the other person goes away enriched. If you take pride away from them in order to feed your own view of yourself, the gift you make —even if it's hours of encouragement and support—

isn't fair compensation. In fact, very often the most giving thing you can do is let someone give to you.

When I was a child I had a friend who had parents who weren't as generous as mine, and often when a group of us went off to swim or play a game she'd disappear without a word. And later we'd find out that she'd spent the day crying on her bed rather than let us know that she lacked the bathing suit or tennis racket to come along. I can't remember how I found this out, or how long it took before I caught on to her. But after a while, whenever she vanished without a word, I'd slip away and get an extra suit, and turn up at her door and flush her out. And after a while she'd dry her tears and come along with us. I never thought about this twice because it was very easy for me to do, never discussed it with her or with anyone else. And it would have been forgotten long ago, if it hadn't happened that we grew up and she got rich about the time that I got poor, and then the relationship was reversed.

It wasn't till then that I discovered how hard it was for me to take, how difficult it is to trust. Or how much power the giver has, and how much control. And when my friend and I had struggled over one restaurant bill too many and I had lost again, I said to her, "Look, we have to talk about this. You've

·80·

made up for the bathing suit over and over again, and I consider myself paid back in full." And she said to me, "Bathing suit? What bathing suit? I don't remember any suit. I just know I give you what I have to give, and wish that I had more, and you give me something that I can't get elsewhere at any price at all."

It takes great generosity to accept generosity, far more than it does to give, so for many of us it is very hard to do. But we must keep in mind that it isn't possible to find yourself in yourself. We find ourselves in others, and in loving and caring for them, we love and care for ourselves. So if taking care of each other is what makes us human, we must share the privilege.

10

Loneliness is something you do to yourself

There seem to be three main streams to life—the emotional, the sensual, and the rational—and all of us are made up of these three, although in differing amounts. There are artists whose lives are lived solely through their emotions and their senses, and accountants and scholars who rein their bodies and feelings with their minds. And there are people whose only sensuality is their self-flagellation, and those who don't know what they feel, only what they think.

I don't know how we become lopsided or what causes one skein in the braid to become thicker than the rest—whether we back away from what we are afraid of, or go with the part of us that functions best. I only know that most people grow more in one way than in others, and the side of them which is the most developed determines their life. And because this is the case, the side of them which is the most developed also dictates the kind of friend they make.

There are friends who feed the spirit, and those who feed the senses, and some with whom the attachment is emotional and warm. And you can be different with each of them, so it makes sense to choose one's friends for the different sides of yourself that you want to express. It is in the choice of friends that we decide what we shall feed and what we are willing to let starve.

I know there are lots of people who believe in one best friend, but I have always found it best to have four or five. You don't want more friends than you can comfortably go to the wall for, should they all call on the same afternoon, but because in any year one of them might be falling in love, getting married, or taking a trip, you should have enough so there will always be three or four around.

Friends are people who help you be more yourself, more the person you are intended to be, and it is possible that without them we don't recognize ourselves, or grow to be what it is in us to be. Our lives are in fact many lives, and we can all be much more than we are, so there cannot be any doubt that the secret of who we become is whom we meet along the way.

Our society isn't very big on friendship, really. We think of friends as people to spend time with when there isn't anyone else around who really matters. And sometimes when we have a vacancy for lover or spouse, we look for someone to fill that slot instead of seeing what there is, and miss what might have been.

There are many sources of friendship which we reject, many potential friends whom we don't see, and hence there are many ways of enriching our lives which we overlook, many sources of love which we turn down.

We rarely think of older people as potential friends, or younger ones, or children or dogs, and friends with exotic backgrounds are considered strange. And should you have a friend who has more or less money than you, you are both immediately suspect.

Men are rarely friends with other men, although they may have male friends with whom they joust. And we certainly don't encourage friendship between men and women—nonsexual unions are considered positively odd. Even women have only recently started to find the way to other women, and with luck that will continue to grow, but friendship in our society is still very much an undeveloped resource.

We tend to think of emotional connections as being limited to certain kinds and feel that friends, like mates, must be the age and sex prescribed. And even when we allow ourselves one best friend, we are always on the alert to be sure they don't interfere with the time meant for our spouse.

If I were to marry again tomorrow, I wouldn't give up one friend. I'd take them all with me as a sort of dowry and tell my new husband that he was getting a rich wife. It takes a long time to understand that there is no relationship which is all-supporting, only those which help you grow stronger in yourself. So a lot of people never realize how important it is to have real friends or how crucial they can be even if you have a mate.

Men are just starting now to understand that women can be many more things to them than partners in the bed. And they are just beginning to see that they can go to women to express feelings they once had to keep to themselves in the man's world in which they dwell, where toughness is equated with not caring and having feelings with breaking down. And women, liberated finally by adequate birth control and economic freedom of a sort, are now able to choose their associates from a broader base. So a growing number of them have started getting many of their needs met through women friends, who understand without being asked.

I find people actively involved in the sexual search don't make very good friends, nor do those who have just fallen in love. A friend has to be someone who values you as much as they value a person with whom they might sleep, and they don't rush off leaving you with a half-eaten steak the moment someone calls to make a date. Too many people put a premium on sexual relationships, thereby discounting friends, and they speak of relationships which don't involve bed as "platonic" and rush to point out that someone is "only a friend." But sex is just a temporary anesthetic against loneliness, and when it is over you still need people with whom you can talk. So if you organize your life in a sequence of short delights with people interchangeably chosen to help you make better love to yourself, you will find before very long that you've used yourself up.

A girl once happened to say to me that she "didn't sleep with her friends," and it struck me how odd a turn of phrase that was. One had to wonder if that meant that she considered the people with whom she did go to bed to be her enemies. Friends are the people who pick you up when someone knocks you down, and help you lick your wounds when love goes awry, so they are the ones who love you, not the other way around, and if you find that you are putting most of your energy into people who put you down rather than into those who build you up, it is certainly time to ask yourself who loves you and who does not.

There is much to be said for friendship. Often friendship offers things that love affairs and marriage don't provide, like honesty and fewer demands, and time off from the fray. There used to be a politician who dropped into my house many nights and sat himself down in a chair and told me all the things that had happened to him that day. And finally I asked him why he came to talk to me each night and why he didn't tell his stories instead to the woman who was his wife, and he answered that it was because he could tell them to me and then leave, and not have to discuss them again, and then he added with a smile, "And I can also tell you the ones in which I don't come out so well."

I know many people worry about sharing their spouse and fear that friendships that are too close take away from them, but I'm almost certain that if we had more friendships we'd have fewer marriages which break up, and a lot of mates who might have strayed before would be content to remain at home. Friendships make marriages more stable by giving the partners a place to air their ambivalences without threatening anyone. And when you can tell a friend something that you feel, you don't mind as much if it isn't understood at home.

One of my friends once said to me, "I get along better with Calvin because I have you," and then we both laughed because it somehow seemed so odd that women could help each other to love men better, but it is nevertheless true. Ever since women have stopped expecting men to rescue them from their uncertainties and begun to think about saving themselves, they have liked men better because they've needed them less, and they've come to love the women who helped them accomplish this.

I wish that men understood better the value of friendship as women are coming to know it now, because too often they still see other people as things to be conquered or held off. Men have allies and they have enemies, but only a few of them really have friends, and marriages would be much stronger if that were not the case.

We are an achievement-oriented society, so a lot

of men put their energy into getting ahead and being a success, postponing closeness with other human beings as if it were a luxury they couldn't afford just yet, and they complain a lot about all the work there is to do as if the priorities were set by someone else. And many of them think of fulfillment as something to be found in money, wealth, success, and applause and don't learn until it's too late that the only wealth that really counts is having loving friends.

11

Some terrible things are done in the name of love

Some time ago, a network executive went to a party and met a pretty girl who was an aspiring television journalist, swimming in the pool. Carried away by the moment, he hired her to be the hostess of a prime-time public affairs show that was his network's flagship. It was the kind of job everyone in television dreams of, and she was no exception, even though she was somewhat skeptical of dreams which are answered at parties and had not expected hers to be answered so soon. Nevertheless, she accepted his offer and made the necessary plans to give up the job she had and to provide for her small daughter so that she would be free to make the trip to the new station eighteen miles away. And she arrived there on the first day of the new season, very excited and bursting with hope, to find that nobody knew what she was to do, and most of them didn't want to know, because they, like her, were suspicious of girls who were hired at parties and guessed the worst about her relationship with the network boss.

It took several months of sitting by her desk waiting for the chance to go on that never came, and several months of lunches eaten all alone while the others went off to the cafeteria without her, and a lot of long drives up the thruway in the morning when she couldn't keep herself from crying, before she accepted the inevitable and asked the network to pay her out. They gladly did, asking only that she return the clothes that the network executive had had someone design for her, and that she give no interviews to the press.

There were several months after that in which she was unemployed, difficult months for a young woman with a child and a housekeeper, to say nothing of a hungry dog to support, and then she lucked out and a newspaper made her its feature writer and she was on her feet again.

It was about a year before she saw the network executive again, and then they met at the same house where they'd met the first time. And again it was in the wee hours of the morning after a big party, but this time she wasn't in the pool. She was coming down the stairs with her coat, and seeing him sitting at the bottom of the stairs talking to someone, she tried to slip by him without being seen. But as she was tiptoeing by, he put his hand on her ankle and said, "Come sit by me awhile. I have something to say to you, something I should have said a long time ago." Then he looked up and said, "I have been reading your stuff in the paper. It's good. You're a fine little writer. I am sorry it didn't work out for you at the station. It should have. You have what it takes."

She said nothing, knowing he hadn't finished, and soon after he added, "I suppose you wonder why I hired you and then abandoned you without giving you a chance. I can tell you if you want to know. The day I came to your house with the contract for you to sign, you were sitting on your front porch, wearing a little summer dress and swinging your legs. And I took one look and I knew if I stayed there for more than just a very few minutes I would fall in love with you, and that I had no choice but to run for my life."

He was pleased with himself when he told her that, pleased with his confession, pleased with this moment they were sharing, and for a moment she was pleased too, pleased to understand at last, pleased to have a compliment where there had been only anguish and confusion before, pleased as somebody is supposed to be when someone makes you a declaration of love. And then she remembered all those mornings driving up the thruway crying, and all the months of not having any money and not knowing what to tell her friends. And she turned to him and said, "I don't think you could have done me much more harm if you had hated me. How odd that you should think of that as love."

Some terrible things are done in the name of love, and some of the worst of them are done by men who let their fantasies run away with them, and by women who unwittingly play into them. I'd like to think such events occur less often today as women are now more vocal about their rights, and hence harder to reduce to stereotypes, but somehow I suspect they still happen too much, because I know how hard such games are to give up, and how often those who play them do not know how much they hurt.

There used to be a married man who spent a lot of time hanging around a friend of mine's house, but who couldn't be reached when she needed him, not until after one birthday celebration, when we held dinner two hours longer than we should have, waiting for him to arrive. And then the next day when he came to tell her why he hadn't made it the night before, she interrupted him in mid-excuse, interrupted him with this burst of words, "Give me your

· 93 ·

home number or leave at once." And when he looked at her with frightened eyes, she said, "I will not call it unless I have cause, but if you value me and want me to survive, you will not expect me to protect your vulnerability at the expense of my own. I respect your privacy and would not easily choose to interfere with that, but you should know my sanity means as much to me as yours, more in fact."

I tell you this story because I wanted to say that sometimes it takes a long time to see the obvious when you have always assumed something can't be changed, and because I wanted you to know he gave her his number without thinking twice, and she is still his friend today, although he no longer has a wife.

There have been times for almost every one of us when things weren't the way we'd wish them to be, times when we've said to ourselves in a whisper, "I deserve much better. Why is there nothing but this for me?" And most of us have tried to make ourselves accept what we don't like, and make the best of what's at hand, and sometimes that is all to the good. But what I am trying to say now is this—if you don't run after loneliness, you don't catch it. And it is a highly communicable disease, so

no one can blame you for drawing a clear line between self-preservation and self-sacrifice, and drawing it early before you are down on your knees.

I had a colleague once who asked if
he might come and spend a weekend with me to
discuss some new developments in his career. And
when I said he was most welcome but that there was
a party I had to go to on Saturday night and hoped
he would come along, he said he didn't think he
should, adding in an awkward voice, "because of
what people might think." And when I asked if his
wife knew about his plans to visit me, and heard that
certainly she did, I asked him whom we were lying
to then. And after a while he acknowledged that he
didn't know himself.

There are so many situations when others treat us
in ways that are not quite right but which we go
along with, although we could change them if we
wanted to enough. I used to let married men keep
their wives insecure by their association with me,
but I don't let that happen anymore. If a husband
comes to talk to me at a party, I make sure I also go
soon after and talk to his wife. And once when a man
whom I dearly loved, but who had a lady he assured
me was very insecure, spent an evening running back

and forth between us in broad view of everyone else, the next morning I called him and said right out, "I don't like this arrangement. It gives you too much power over both of us." And then I gave him fair warning that I meant to invite the two of them to dinner and hoped he would encourage her to come. And they came to dinner and are still coming today, and her friendship means as much to me now as does his.

Old patterns die hard, but we must help them die if they do not serve us well, and men and women must be friends before this war can end. I know it isn't always easy to recognize how we preserve the old ways and keep them alive, but men and women who feel guilty about being friends always keep each other insecure.

It is not easy for women to be friends with men, since many men simply don't understand that there are several kinds of relationships you can have with women—and sleeping with them, or wishing you could, is not all there is. Some people say a woman can only be friends with a man who has no interest in her, or has a wife he doesn't want to hurt, but although it seems that way sometimes, I do not think that need be true. A woman can point out the other ways men might relate to her. What happens between two people is as much the decision of two as it is of one.

I remember a man who once called on a friend on a Sunday afternoon, claiming he had to see her and that he could not wait. And when he arrived he said he'd been wrestling with the idea of her for too many nights and now he'd decided to face it out. And she smiled at him while she thought of the life she'd planned for herself, and then she said, "Suppose I make you a counter-offer. You are at a stage when you want to have a fling, to take a chance, to shake up your life, and I need to lie low and be quiet so I can work. Therefore we are out of sync. But I am willing to be your friend, and that's an offer you shouldn't refuse, because it's much easier to find someone to run off with than it is to find a friend, and a friend is worth a whole lot more in the end."

I know that our society isn't set up for a woman to be friends with a man, and that when a man is looking for a lover or a wife it is not easy to change his mind. But I know also that you can't run off with everyone who's on the loose, and that a man who is your friend will stay longer and treat you better than one who feels guilty about what he does. And I also know that many of the men who claim they have to see you urgently have a wife who's just gone away for three weeks and in three weeks she'll be back.

There is a difference between loneliness and aloneness and lonesomeness, and loneliness is something you do to yourself. And those who pack loneliness in their luggage carry it around with them wherever they go. We have only so much emotional currency, it isn't an unlimited supply, so you've got to invest it wisely if you want to make it grow.

12

In a full heart there is room for everything

I wish I could claim that all the people whom I have loved have always loved me back, or that my needs and those of the people closest to me have always dovetailed perfectly. But friendship doesn't work that way, and people's needs aren't always the same, so it is only fair to say that I have often wished for more, or wished for something no one had to give, and in that I know I am not alone.

Some people feel angry when they think of moments when they've had to stand alone, and question the value they once put upon friends who weren't there when they needed them. But I think the thing to remember is this—you don't get from friends what you give to them, you get what they have to give, and that is the thing you must not forget. People can only give you what they have to give.

It is difficult to remember this when you know just what you need and none of your friends have it to give, and especially difficult when you have given it to them in the past. But you will save yourself a lot of grief if you keep in mind that you don't have you for a friend, however much you might wish you did. You have that person out there instead.

Perhaps you will take chicken soup to a friend who is sick, and they will forget your birthday just the same. Or maybe you will have them to your parties and they will give none to which you might be asked. But maybe they will hand you a piece of truth one day, in a sentence tossed off with a sidelong glance, and if it's something you couldn't have found inside yourself, you will have been repaid in full.

It helps to remember too that the corollary of a person's good qualities is usually the bad—which means nice guys can't get cabs—and to recognize as well that the best characteristics of a friend usually have to be paid for at the other end. Most of us spend a lot of time being vexed by qualities in people which are the flip side of those we like about them best. The child-like and vulnerable part of someone draws us while the passive, indecisive part makes us wish we'd stayed away.

But you have to bear in mind, if somebody is particularly sensitive and understands everything you feel, you might have to hold their hand a lot when the world does them in. And if you know a take-charge person whom you can surrender your life to when it gets too much for you, you are likely to find yourself having trouble wrenching it back again after they are through.

People are friends in spots. There are usually qualities in a person you would like to be-friend, and parts you don't want to have anything to do with at all, and you must learn to be grateful for what is there for you and not annoyed by what can never be.

There are people who make good friends and bad acquaintances and people with whom one loves to banter but wouldn't want to cry. And perhaps we have to learn which is which and that you don't need a lot of people to play tennis with if what you hunger for is a companion for your inner life.

There are so many parts of us that have to communicate with parts of another person that we each need several people to unlock all the chambers of our heart. And while we have all been conditioned to hunger for the one person who gives us everything and gives it to us all of the time, it helps to accept that life doesn't consist of total people. It consists of moments, moments which are gifts that you can pick up and hang like pearls around your neck, but no one will hand them to you. You have to supply the string in order to hug them to yourself.

There is a lot to be said for reduced expectations, and a lot to be said for accepting the limitations of friends. Because once you understand that there is no love which assuages all hurt, it is as though you have walked all night in a haunted woods and stumbled out again into the light. And after that you are more contented and more easily pleased by life. And when love happens, be it for a minute or for a week, you view it as a gift, as you would view the sun coming out in a cloudy sky, and you are grateful for the moment, not angry that there are so few.

"But," I hear you saying, "surely friendship is supposed to be having someone in your camp, someone who is there when you need them, no matter what. And if I can't count on my friends when I need them, then I have no friends really, and nobody loves me. No amount of pretty phrases will make me believe otherwise. If no one is prepared to answer my call, I am simply a cheap date, an easy lay, someone to rip off."

I can hear you asking this because I have asked it too, and I don't have any answer for you except to pass on what it took me so long to learn. We are all essentially alone, and sometimes the people whom you love can make it through, and sometimes they can't get to you no matter how much they try.

People's perceptions are not the same, and therefore what often looks very clear to one may not look as clear to another set of eyes. So much of what you see depends on where you are standing when you look. In human relationships one knows what one gives out, but never what is received, so it is possible that a friend's prescription may not work on your complaint. And it is also true that friends, even the very best, have a cut-off point, a point at which they must beg off to protect themselves—even if this means that they save themselves at the expense of you.

The friend who saw you through your tragic love affair might not be able to see you through a serious illness, or the loss of a child. And even when they want to help, people often don't know what to do, so they proffer a tangerine for your nervous breakdown and, overcome with a sense of their own inadequacy, turn tail and leave you on your own. And sometimes they try to jolly you out of things because they can't take the strain of seeing you upset, or demand that you tell them all the details and then leave when they feel they can't take any more, failing to comprehend that they've done nothing for you at all, except maybe tire you out.

There is a parable which was written a long time ago about three men who were sent on a very important mission. And the first man didn't make it because his horse broke a leg, and the second man didn't make it because he was ambushed and was wounded in the neck, and the third man arrived late, covered with blood, and apologized for the delay, saying in his defense only that it had taken him longer than he'd hoped because he'd been captured, and as he'd lost his horse he'd had no choice but to walk the rest of the way.

I tell you this story because I wanted to say there are so many ways to beg off in life and still believe that you have done everything humanly possible that some people even fool themselves. And I wanted you to keep that in mind in case there is ever a time when you are disappointed in friendship or a friend.

Some people beg off early, and some people beg off late, and a very few of them keep on coming no matter what happens along the way. But the thing you must never forget is this—when you don't expect anything you always get back a lot.

"It is in the thirties that we want friends," Scott Fitzgerald said. "In the forties, we know that they won't save us any more than love did." And perhaps he was right. But what he didn't say is that we mustn't expect them to. We must save ourselves. And while I know a lot of people have suggested, as Kipling did, that "He travels the fastest who travels alone," where are we going, I want to know? And if the answer is where I think, Carl Sandburg came closer to the mark when he wrote, "The dead clutch in their clenched fist only what they have managed to give away." There is only the past, the present, and the perhaps, and the love that passes through us on the way.

The people in one's life are like the pillars on one's porch you see life through. And sometimes they hold you up, and sometimes they lean on you, and sometimes it is just enough to know they're standing by.

ABOUT THE AUTHOR

MERLE SHAIN is a communicator. She works as a writer (both of books and screenplays as well as magazine articles and newspaper pieces) and as a broadcaster (in both radio and television). She is a popular speaker making speeches and leading seminars regularly in the United States and Canada. She began her career in the media with a radio series on "The Changing Role of Women to the Learning Stage," which she wrote, researched, edited and broadcast for the CBC. Since then she has become a widely acclaimed television host, interviewer, critic and talk show guest. In 1968 she was an aide to Pierre Elliott Trudeau during his successful bid for the leadership of the Liberal party in Canada, working as a creative associate in charge of visual design, convention programming and personnel training. Her first book was *Some Men Are More Perfect Than Others,* which became a national bestseller. She has been married and has a son, and lives in London.